CAERLEON AND THE ROMAN ARMY

Roman Legionary Museum: a guide

by

Richard J Brewer

First Published 1987
Second Edition 2000
by the
National Museums & Galleries of Wales
Cathays Park
Cardiff CF10 3NP

ISBN 0 7200 0488 8

Designed by Dragonfly Design
Printed in Great Britain by The Westdale Press Ltd

Acknowledgements
The second edition of this guide has been produced with considerable help from Julie Reynolds, Roman Legionary Museum Caerleon, Evan Chapman and Edward Besly, Department of Archaeology & Numismatics. Thanks are due to Kevin Thomas and Jim Wild, Photographic Department, NMGW, who undertook most of the photography and Tony Daly, Department of Archaeology & Numismatics, who produced the illustrations. I am also grateful to those who have given permission for their photographs to be reproduced and these are credited with the images. Arwel Hughes and Elin ap Hywel, Publications and Design, NMGW, were responsible for overseeing production of the English and Welsh versions of this guide. Finally, I wish to acknowledge the efforts of Chris Haines and the Ermine Street Guard who bring the Roman army alive at Caerleon and other historic sites and museums in this country and abroad.

CAERLEON
AND THE
ROMAN
ARMY

CONTENTS

CAERLEON-*ISCA*

CAERLEON, 'City of the Legion', stands on the right bank of the Usk, and was known to the Romans as *Isca* after the river. Established in AD 74 or 75, *Isca* was one of the three permanent legionary bases in Roman Britain; the other two were at Chester (*Deva*) and York (*Eburacum*).

The fortress was of playing-card shape, and covered an area of 20.5 ha (50 acres). It contained all the buildings necessary for the accommodation, administration, provision and welfare of the legion – barracks for the men, a palace for the legate, houses for the officers, workshops, granaries, large baths and even a hospital. All was defended by a ditch and a walled rampart, with regularly-spaced watch towers and imposing gateways.

Its garrison, as inscriptions tell us, was *legio II Augusta*, a body of heavy infantry comprising well over 5,000 men, all Roman citizens. Beyond the defences lay the Amphitheatre and parade ground, the civil settlements and the cemeteries.

On the departure of the legion from Caerleon in about AD 290, much of the fortress was systematically demolished. This, together with the robbing of stone from medieval times onwards, reduced the Roman building remains to below ground level, except for a few stretches of the fortress-wall. A lack of modern overbuilding – certainly in comparison with York and Chester – has allowed large-scale exploration by archaeologists, and much of the plan of the stone fortress has been recovered as a result.

Caerleon has yielded, partly by chance but mainly by archaeological excavation, a rich collection of Roman finds. On display in the Museum are sculptures, inscriptions, tombstones, building materials, a labyrinth mosaic, military equipment, pottery, glass and jewellery – including a remarkable collection of engraved gemstones from the Fortress Baths. An important series of Roman objects from the predecessor of *Isca* – the fortress at Usk (*Burrium*) excavated between 1965 and 1976 – is also exhibited.

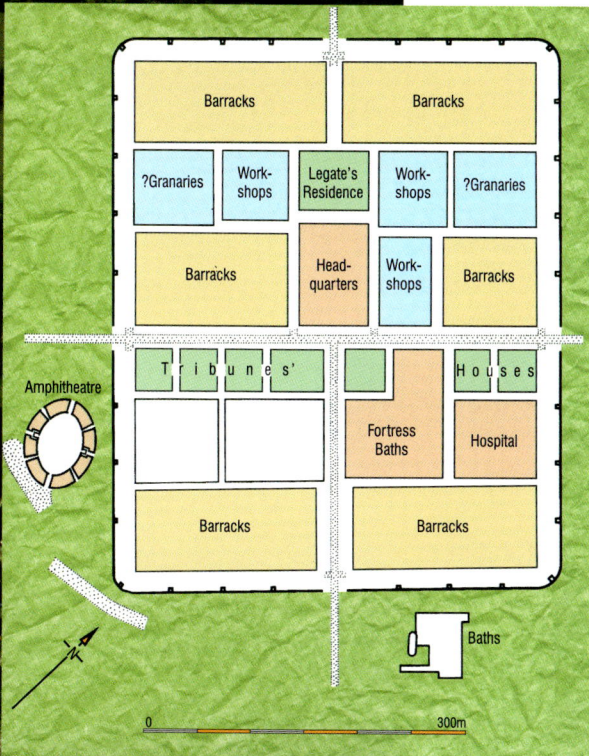

Barracks

Barracks

?Granaries | Work-shops | Legate's Residence | Work-shops | ?Granaries

Barracks | Head-quarters | Work-shops | Barracks

Tribunes' | Houses

Amphitheatre

Fortress Baths | Hospital

Barracks | Barracks

Baths

0 | 300m

THE MUSEUM OF ANTIQUITIES

T HE FIRST excavations at Caerleon took place in the 1840s, adding their relics to others produced by chance from as far back as 1602. This upsurge of archaeological endeavour led in 1847 to the formation of the Caerleon (now the Monmouthshire) Antiquarian Association with the object of founding a museum to house the inscriptions and other Roman finds from the legionary fortress.

John Edward Lee (1808-87).
From 1841 until his retirement to Torquay in 1868 he was active in Monmouthshire, both as an industrialist and as an antiquary. Lee was the inspiration behind the formation of the Caerleon Antiquarian Association and the Museum of Antiquities.
(Torquay Natural History Society)

In 1862, Lee published **Isca Silurum; or an Illustrated Catalogue of the Museum of Antiquities at Caerleon.** *All the illustrations, by Lee, were of a very high quality. This plate illustrates two ivory carvings, probably from a burial.*

Sir Digby Mackworth, Bart., first President of the Association and a considerable landowner in Caerleon, offered a suitable plot of land for the building at a peppercorn rent, and also made a generous donation of money and materials. In June 1848, a local builder was instructed to proceed with the construction of the Museum at an estimated cost of £407. On the 2 August 1850, the Museum of Antiquities was opened to the public.

A particularly distinguished name in Caerleon archaeology is that of John Edward Lee (1808-87), a Yorkshireman, who settled in Caerleon in 1841 having joined a firm of iron-manufacturers in Newport. Lee devoted his leisure to learned pursuits, mainly archaeology and geology. Concerned to record Caerleon's Roman heritage, he produced in 1845 *Delineations of Roman Antiquities found at Caerleon and the Neighbourhood*, illustrated – as were all his works – by his own hand. It was largely through Lee's efforts that the Museum was established, and his most important work was *Isca Silurum* (1862), a catalogue of the collections.

Lee also participated in the first archaeological investigation of any significance, when in 1849-50 he undertook the recording of the remains of a large Roman building (later identified as a bath-house), lying outside the east corner of the fortress on the site of the medieval castle. His involvement in Caerleon ended in 1868, when he moved for the sake of his wife's health to Torquay.

In 1930 the Museum of Antiquities was handed over by the Association to the National Museum of Wales, and was renamed 'The Legionary Museum of Caerleon'. However, even the care of the National Museum could not preserve the old building for ever, and in 1983 the decision was taken to replace it with a larger, well-equipped museum worthy of the site and collection.

The new Museum retains the Doric porch of its predecessor, a much loved element of the Caerleon townscape. The Roman Legionary Museum was re-opened officially by His Royal Highness the Duke of Gloucester in June 1987. Since then it has become an active archaeological centre and proved immensely popular with visitors. More recently, the Capricorn Centre, an acclaimed educational facility with a reconstructed barrack room, and the Pegasus Centre have been added.

The Museum of Antiquities, about 1850. From a lithograph by J F Mullock of Newport.

Antiquarian Museum.

REVEALING THE PAST

THE PICTURE that we have of the Roman fortress of *Isca* comes almost entirely from archaeological investigation. The first excavations that can be called scientific took place in 1908-9, and were followed in 1926-7 by the exploration of 'King Arthur's Round Table', the Amphitheatre, by Dr (later Sir) Mortimer and Mrs T V Wheeler – an early instance of a sponsored excavation, which was financed by the *Daily Mail*. It is still the most fully-excavated amphitheatre of Roman Britain.

Excavation of the Amphitheatre in progress, 1927. The task involved the digging and cartage of nearly 30,000 tons of soil at a total cost of less than £3,000. Today, the Amphitheatre is in the care of the National Assembly for Wales, acting through Cadw: Welsh Historic Monuments.

Lying as it does on the outskirts of the growing town of Newport, there has been (and still is) much pressure for development at Caerleon. Allowing for interruptions during the Second World War and for most of the 1970s, there have been until recent years almost annual excavations since 1926, both inside and outside the fortress.

The recovery of Roman *Isca* from under modern Caerleon has largely been the fruit of a long partnership between the National Museum of Wales and the Office of Works and its various successors – now Cadw: Welsh Historic Monuments.

In addition to the Amphitheatre, it has been possible to preserve for public display parts of the Fortress Baths, a section of the defences on the south-west side, and in the western corner (Prysg Field), the only legionary barrack-block to be seen in Europe. Most of the excavations, however, have been of a rescue nature, carried out in advance of destruction by building-work.

The technique of excavation and recording during these ninety-odd years has not remained static. For many years sites were normally investigated by cutting narrow, and often deep trenches. However, the introduction of area-excavation in the late 1970s has led to a greater yield of information from sites, especially regarding the deeply-buried timber buildings belonging to the original fortress of AD 74 or 75.

Modern excavations continue to tell us more about the architecture and history of *Isca* and of the daily life of the soldiers of the Second Augustan Legion for whom the place was once home.

Much of the open ground on the western side of the fortress is owned by the nation, and is preserved for future research. Most of the other undeveloped plots are protected by the Ancient Monuments Acts, which prevent any unauthorised disturbance of the ground.

The cold hall (frigidarium) of the Fortress Baths, 1979. The baths were first identified in rescue-work in 1964; excavations undertaken in 1977-9 uncovered the swimming pool and cold hall for public display.

Excavations on the site of the Museum in 1984-5 revealed the house of the camp prefect (praefectus castrorum). The framework of the earliest house, built about AD 75, was entirely of timber; the oak uprights were set in pits and trenches.

A gold piece (aureus) of Claudius (AD 41-54) found at Llanelen, near Abergavenny (loan of Mr R Herbert). Claudius undertook the conquest of Britain in 43, largely because he needed the prestige of a military victory.

Tombstone of Gaius Largennius, originally from Lucca in northern Italy, who served as a soldier in the Second Augustan Legion at Strasbourg on the Upper Rhine before the invasion of Britain. He died at the age of 38 after 17 years' service. (Reproduced by permission of the Musée Archéologique, Strasbourg)

The extent of the Empire in AD 43; also showing the previous fortresses of the legions which came to Britain. The Second Augustan Legion was one of the four legions which formed part of the invasion force.

THE ROMANS ARRIVE

BRITANNIA was one of the last provinces to be added to the Roman Empire, and it proved to be one of the most troublesome. The Romans invaded Britain in AD 43 with an army of about 40,000 men, led by Aulus Plautius. This large force employed four legions – *II Augusta, IX Hispana, XIV Gemina* and *XX Valeria* – with accompanying auxiliary troops.

Landing on the Kentish coast, they won a decisive battle and quickly advanced to the River Thames, near London. They awaited the arrival of the Emperor Claudius before marching on the British stronghold at Colchester (*Camulodunum*). There the defeated tribal leaders submitted to the Romans, and others who wished to be Roman allies negotiated peaceful settlements. Within a few years the new province covered all of south-eastern Britain.

By 48 Roman forces were on the borders of what is now Wales. The two most powerful tribes in Wales – the Silures in the south-east and the Ordovices in the north – were bitterly hostile to the Romans, and an arduous struggle, lasting nearly three decades, was to ensue. Until 51, the heroic resistance was led by the refugee British leader Caratacus, but it was in the year following his capture that the Roman army suffered its greatest defeat in Britain, when a large part of a legion was lost in a battle with the Silures.

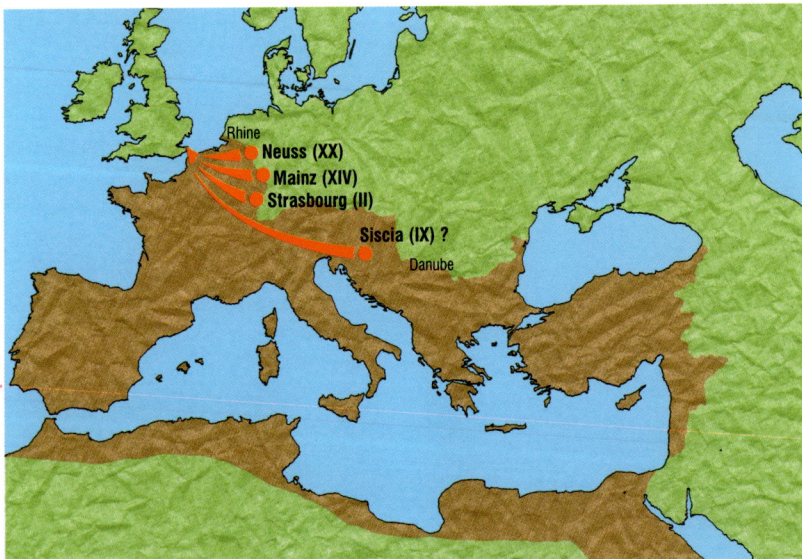

USK: AN EARLY FORTRESS

DESPITE the early setbacks and severe losses, the Emperor Nero continued the aggressive policy against the Welsh tribes. During the governorship of Didius Gallus (52-7), the Roman army pushed into eastern Wales and the southern coastal belt.

A brass dupondius of Nero (54-68). The emperor maintained an aggressive policy against the Welsh tribes.

To consolidate these advances legionary fortresses were established at Wroxeter and Usk, as well as a string of forts running the length of the Welsh Marches and with others forward of this line.

From 58-60, the governor Suetonius Paulinus conducted successful campaigns in both

An aerial view of Usk. The fortress occupied a strategic position in the Usk Valley, the main route to the uplands of southern Wales. The site of the fortress proved to be a bad choice for it was subject to flash-floods.
(Royal Commission on the Ancient and Historical Monuments of Wales. Crown Copyright)

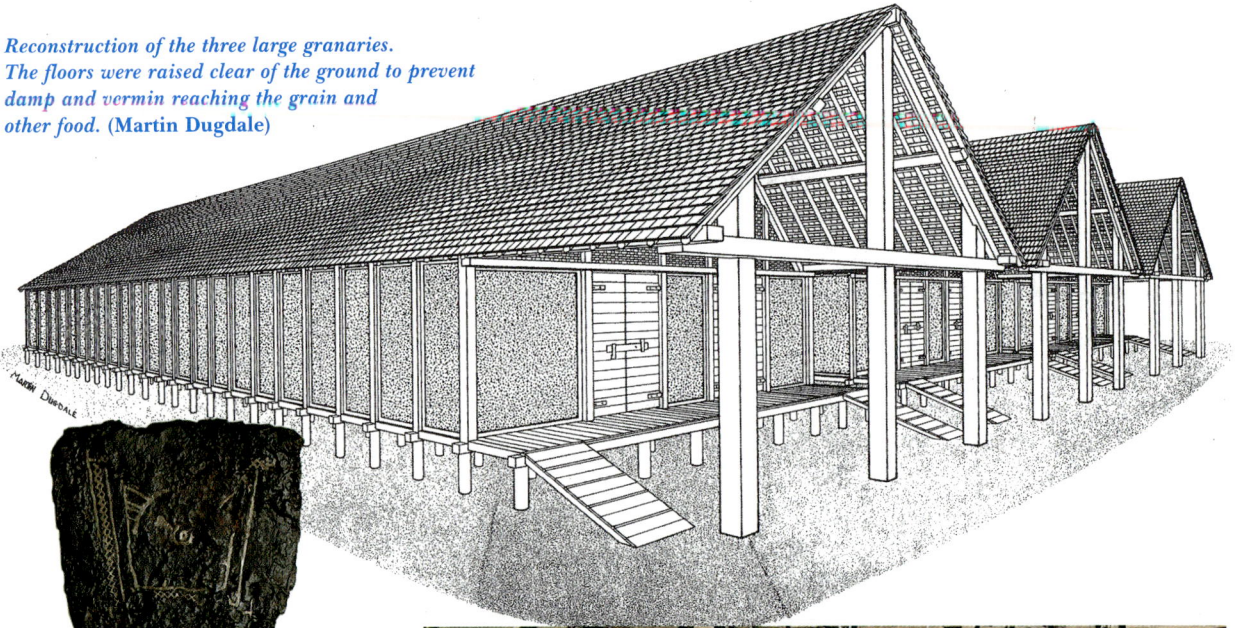

south and north Wales, and the Roman army was on the verge of complete victory when disaster struck. Paulinus was forced to withdraw to combat the rebellion raised by Boudicca, Queen of the

The large granaries of the fortress sited just inside the east gate, during excavation in 1969. Each of the three buildings consisted of a grid of 225 posts set in 25 trenches spaced 1.5 m apart.

A soldier's iron dagger-sheath inlaid with silver wire, mid-first century AD.

Copper alloy harness-stud decorated with rings of inlaid glass mosaic, second century AD. Found before 1862. An exact twin from Chepstow (18 km away) is in the British Museum.

Brooches of the mid-first century: fan-tail brooch; 'dolphin' brooch; 'Hod Hill' type brooch with tinned surface. Brooches were worn to fasten cloaks and other garments.

Iceni (Norfolk). The conquest of Wales had to be postponed for over a decade while the ravaged province underwent reconstruction.

The presence of an early legionary fortress at Usk (*Burrium*) was detected only as recently as the late 1960s.

It was built about the year 55, probably by the Twentieth Legion as a base for the conquest of south Wales. The fortress covered an area of 19.5 ha (48 acres) and was defended by a rampart, with timber towers and gateways, and a ditch in front.

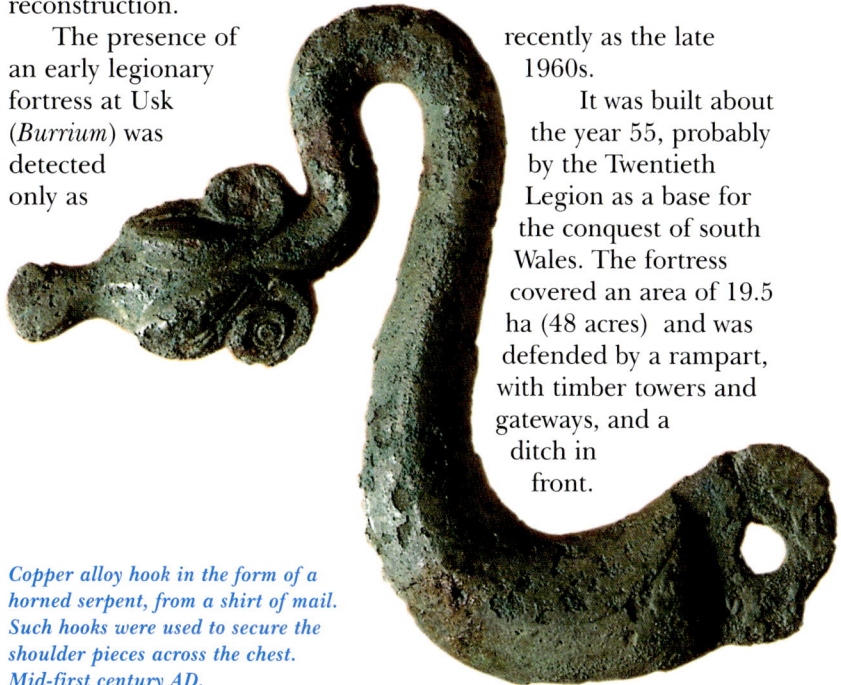

Copper alloy hook in the form of a horned serpent, from a shirt of mail. Such hooks were used to secure the shoulder pieces across the chest. Mid-first century AD.

A mould-blown glass cup of the first century AD. A wide variety of tablewares, drinking cups and vessels for serving liquids and foods, were in use during the life of the fortress.

The garrison at Usk required huge quantities of kitchen and tablewares. Much of the pottery was produced close to the fortress, probably by civilian potters some of whom may have come from the Rhineland. The remainder was supplied by establishments elsewhere in Britain and on the Continent.

Large-scale excavations, conducted between 1965 and 1976, were concentrated along the main street linking the east and west gates of the fortress. They revealed details of roads, two groups of granaries – used to store grain and other provisions to feed the large invasion force – stores, a workshop, and part of an officer's house, all built of wood.

Usk was vacated by the Twentieth Legion in the late 60s, but demolition did not proceed immediately, and the base continued to be held by a caretaker garrison. The fortress was dismantled only when new headquarters were built in AD 74 or 75 by the Second Augustan Legion, downstream at Caerleon. Soon after, a smaller auxiliary fort was established on the site.

Copper alloy seal-box lid (x2) with a charging boar, the emblem of the Twentieth Legion.

CAERLEON: THE FIRST FORTRESS

Silver **denarius** *of the Emperor Vespasian (69-79). He had commanded the Second Augustan Legion with distinction during the early days of the conquest of Britain.* **(Not from Caerleon)**

The military network soon after the conquest. About the year 78 the garrison of Wales amounted nominally to more than 30,000 men. Nothing like that number could be maintained indefinitely, and forts were phased out wherever possible, more especially as the occupation of northern Britain brought additional demands.

UNDER the Emperor Vespasian there was a new determination, and Julius Frontinus, provincial governor from 74-7, was appointed to complete the subjugation of the Welsh tribes. He led the Second Augustan Legion to their new fortress at Caerleon and forward to complete the defeat of the Silures. In mid- and north Wales, the Ordovices were likewise subdued after campaigns by Frontinus and by his successor Agricola in 78.

About 36 auxiliary units – infantry and part-mounted cohorts 500 and 1,000 strong, and cavalry regiments 500 strong – operating from a network of forts, were needed to police the new territory. These units were dependent according to their location on the two new legionary fortresses, Caerleon and Chester; the latter being at first the base of the Second Adiutrix, replaced in about 86 by the Twentieth. In the early days, the First Thracian cavalry regiment *(Ala I Thracum)* may have been garrisoned with the legion at Caerleon, adding a strong cavalry element to its capabilities.

Very little is known about the plan of the first fortress, for the remains of the earliest structures lie deeply buried beneath later deposits and have largely gone undetected until recent years.

Five gold pieces **(aurei)***, the latest of AD 74; possibly a soldier's savings hidden inside the fortress shortly after the legion's arrival.*

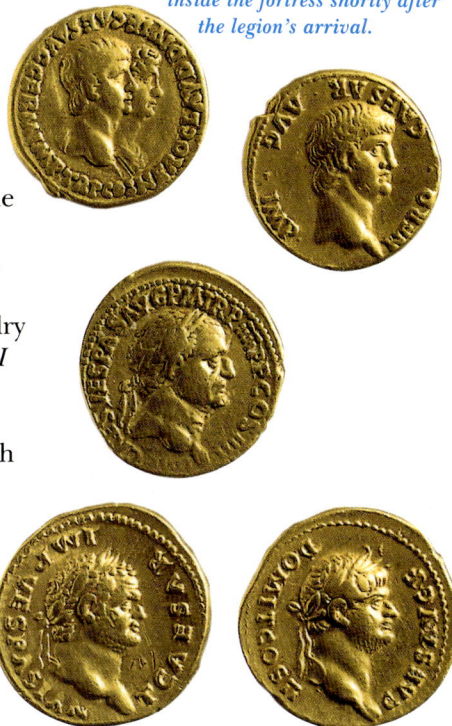

Legionary fortress
Legionary fortress evacuated
Auxiliary fort
Fortlet

SEGONTIUM
DEVA LEG.II ADIUTRIX
VIRICONIUM
GLEVUM
ISCA LEG.II AUG

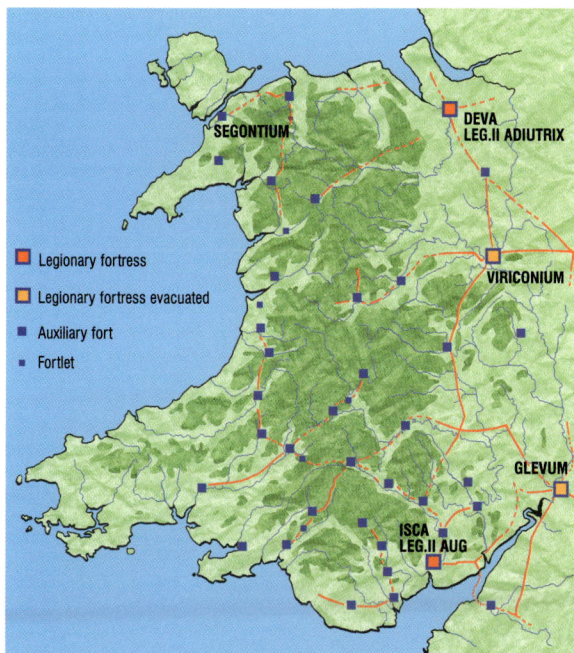

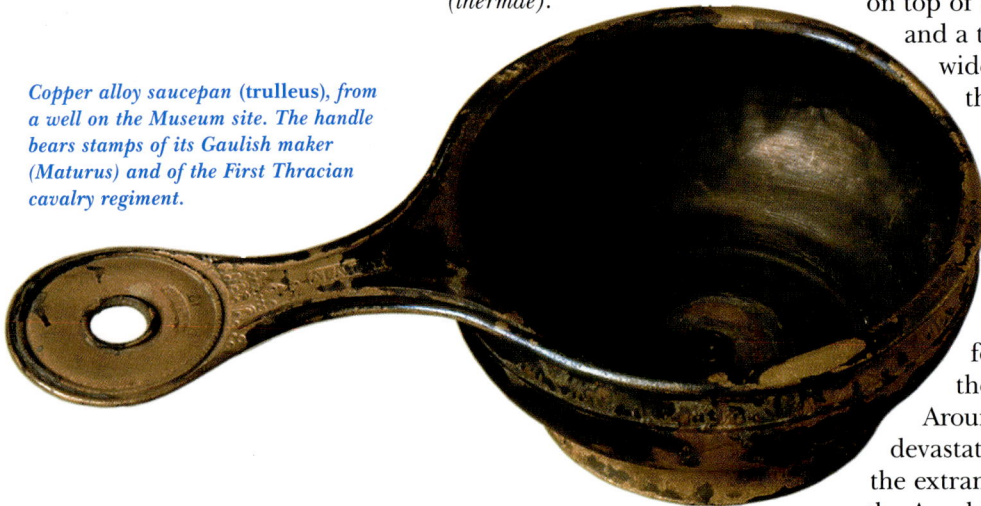

An oak post set in a trench. Part of a timber building, the residence of the camp prefect, excavated beneath the site of the Museum. The first buildings within the fortress, with rare exceptions – notably the Fortress Baths and the fabrica (a large workshop) – were constructed of timber.

The barracks and many of the other buildings were entirely of timber-framed construction; they are marked only by the trenches and pits which held the uprights of the framework.

Before the end of the first century, the original timbers must have started to rot, for many structures were replaced. The new buildings had cobble footings for the timber superstructure to rest on, in an attempt to alleviate decay. From the outset some buildings were constructed in masonry throughout, such as the elaborate Fortress Baths complex (*thermae*).

The original defences, as at Usk, consisted of a single ditch and bank, with timber interval turrets and gateways. There would have been a broad walk on top of the turf-faced rampart, and a timber palisade with wide embrasures. Outside the defences, to the south-west, were the timber sheds possibly of a military supply base. A masonry bath-house was also soon built, and between it and the fortress was squeezed the Amphitheatre.

Around the year 90, a devastating fire swept through the extramural area, engulfing the Amphitheatre and the sheds.

Copper alloy saucepan (trulleus), from a well on the Museum site. The handle bears stamps of its Gaulish maker (Maturus) and of the First Thracian cavalry regiment.

CAERLEON: REBUILDING

T HE FORTRESS was occupied for over 200 years, and there was a need for regular maintenance and at times for extensive rebuilding. Excavation has shown the structural evolution of *Isca* to be extremely complex.

A brass **sestertius** *of the Emperor Trajan (98-117) found at Caerwent.*

Italian marble dedication to the Emperor Trajan. This inscription, erected in AD 100, may have adorned the south-west gate. It is one of extremely few inscriptions of Roman Britain to be cut on marble. Specks of paint remain, indicating that the letters had been coloured in the customary red. The slab seems to have been ordered from Italy with its text ready-cut. The inscription was probably cut in AD 99, but by the time it was set up the Emperor Trajan had entered his third consulship and the consular numeral had to be changed from II to III. Delivery of the inscription may have been delayed because the seas were closed over the winter.

Romans traditionally recorded important building-work by the setting-up of an inscription. These dedications can be closely dated, for they normally bear the name and titles of the reigning emperor. There are several such building records from Caerleon, and these provide an invaluable historical source.

Imp(eratori) Caes(ari) divi [Nervae f(ilio)] / Nervae Traia[no Aug(usto)] / Ger(manico) pontif(ici) maximo [trib(unicia)] / potest(ate) p(atri) p(atriae) / co(n)s(uli) III / leg(io) II Aug(usta)

'To the Emperor Caesar Nerva Trajan Augustus, conqueror of Germany, son of the deified Nerva, high priest, with tribunician power, father of his country, consul for the third time, the Second Augustan Legion (dedicates this).'

Before the end of the first century a strong wall, 1.5 m thick, was added to the fortress-defences, and stone turrets and gateways replaced those of timber. The period 100-20 saw many of the barracks, officers' houses and other buildings replaced, this time with a few courses of masonry to carry the entire timber frame clear of the damp ground. During the second and third centuries the fortress saw many comings and goings, for detachments of the legion were often needed elsewhere.

The south-west gateway, one of the four imposing entrances to the fortress. By the end of the first century, a strong wall was added to the defences, and stone gateways and turrets replaced those of timber.

IMP·CAES·DIVI·NERVAE·F· NERVAE·TRAIANO·AVG· GER·PONTIF·MAXIMO·TRIB· POTEST · P · P · COS · III LEG II AVG

A building inscription cut on a slab of local sandstone and recording the complete reconstruction of barracks for the seventh cohort in about 253-8.

Imp(eratores) Valerianus et Gallienus / Aug(usti) et Valerianus nobilissimus / Caes(ar) cohorti VII centurias a so/lo restituerunt per Desticium Iubam / v(irum) c(larissimum) legatum Aug(ustorum) pr(o) pr(aetore) et / Vitulasium Laetinianum leg(atum) leg(ionis) / II Aug(ustae) curante Domit(io) Potentino / praef(ecto) leg(ionis) eiusdem

'The Emperors Valerian and Gallienus, Augusti, and Valerian, most noble Caesar, restored from ground-level barrack-blocks for the seventh cohort, acting through Desticius Juba, of senatorial rank and governor of the province (Britannia Superior) *and the legate of the Second Augustan Legion, Vitulasius Laetinianus, the legionary prefect, Domitius Potentinus being in charge of the work.'*

At times – such as the periods when the legion was involved in construction work on Hadrian's Wall (122-32 or later) and the Antonine Wall (142-4) – the fortress was only lightly garrisoned. Buildings left vacant may have fallen into disrepair, and their renovation would have been the first task for the returning detachments.

A considerable mass of finds from Caerleon attests a strong occupation in the latter half of the second century. In the third century restoration and maintenance at the fortress is recorded by several inscriptions. The legion, however, was heavily involved in the Emperor Severus's punitive expedition into Scotland, 207-11, and in garrison-duty and reconstruction work throughout the north for some years after.

It appears that the garrison of *Isca* had been reduced to such an extent by about 230 that it was no longer worthwhile firing the great hypocaust heating-system of the Fortress Baths. The latest reconstruction work recorded by inscription is in 274/5. By the end of the third century, the legion had departed, and the fortress was put in the hands of the demolition-gangs.

Fragments of the latest-known imperial dedication from Isca, *naming the Emperor Aurelian (270-5); originally part of a long frieze. It is uncertain which building it adorned. The imperial titles can be restored.*

I]mp(erator) [Caes(ar) L(ucius) Domitius A]urelia[nus P(ius) F(elix) Aug(ustus)

CONSTRUCTION

THE FORTRESS was built and maintained by the soldiers of the Second Augustan Legion. Each legion contained in its ranks a wide range of skilled men including ditch-diggers, surveyors, architects, water engineers, glaziers, brick and roof-tile makers, plumbers, stonecutters, limeburners, woodcutters and carpenters, as well as general labourers.

Supervision of all construction work was the responsibility of the camp prefect *(praefectus castrorum)* – a title changed under Severus (193-211) to legionary prefect *(praefectus legionis)*. Systematic and detailed planning was essential, if barracks for over 5,000 men, headquarters, workshops, stores, hospital, baths, granaries, and all other necessary buildings

Iron tools: masons' hammers and trowel, and carpenters' plane-blade and gouge. Many of the craftsmen's tools resemble those of today.

The Fortress Baths as they may have appeared about AD 80, with the exercise hall shown under construction. Built of stone and concrete, they were the creation of an architect in the forefront of an innovative school of which other early products are baths at Vindonissa and Avenches in Switzerland, and the Baths of Titus in Rome itself, as well as the Second Augustan's baths at its former base at Exeter. (Painting by Paul Jenkins)

Most buildings would have been roofed in heavy tiles; the joints of the flanged **tegulae** *were covered by the semi-cylindrical* **imbrices***. Large quantities of roofing tile and brick were produced by the legion for use in the fortress. The kilns were probably located near the River Usk to make use of the alluvial clay.*

The kilns also produced gable-ornaments (antefixa) bearing protective and evil-averting devices, such as this gorgon's head.

were to be accommodated within the enclosure.

The layout is based on a right-angled partitioning, for which a simple surveying instrument, the *groma* – a cross-staff – was used. Most of the buildings were of simple construction, as has been seen; but a few, such as the headquarters and baths, were immense under-takings. The Fortress Baths were

especially ambitious, being of a novel architectural form, with massive concrete vaults.

Building materials would have been needed in abundance both for the initial construction and for subsequent maintenance and new building-programmes. It has been estimated that the construction of the first fortress would have entailed the felling of 150 ha of woodland, unless, as has been suggested, some timbers were salvaged from the old Usk base and floated down-river for reuse.

The local Old Red Sandstone, quarried by the legion, was used for most masonry work, but some finer stones – such as Purbeck marble from Dorset, and Bath stone from the south side of the Severn – were brought from some distance to decorate the more elaborate buildings. Lias limestone, probably from the beds at

A handsome tablet inscribed 'Century of Rufinius', from the Amphitheatre, late first century AD. Red-lead paint survives in the lettering. This tablet was designed for display unlike most of the roughly-incised 'centurial stones' which were concealed beneath rendering after the work had been passed as satisfactory.

Lliswerry on the eastern outskirts of Newport, was employed in the production of mortar. Lead from the Mendips, and the mines at Draethen to the north of Cardiff, was required for water-pipes and tanks. Most of the buildings would have been roofed in heavy tiles. These were made in the legionary brickworks and tilery (*figlina*), perhaps sited near the river close to the alluvial clays which provided the raw material.

Some buildings had glazed windows, and panes of blue-green glass were probably cast on the spot from scrap bottle- and vessel-glass. Blacksmiths would have manufactured iron nails in abundance (witness the three-quarters of a million abandoned at the short-lived fortress of Inchtuthil, near Perth), as well as hinges, locks, and a large variety of tools.

Some construction work, such as the building of the fortress wall and the Amphitheatre, was carried out by legionaries operating in centurial working-parties. Each gang was responsible for a given section of the building, and marked its labours by inscribing its title on a facing-stone so that the standard of work could be checked. A number of these simple building records have been found at Caerleon.

The practice of marking officially-produced bricks and tiles was introduced by the legionary authorities in about AD 100, to regulate their use and prevent theft.

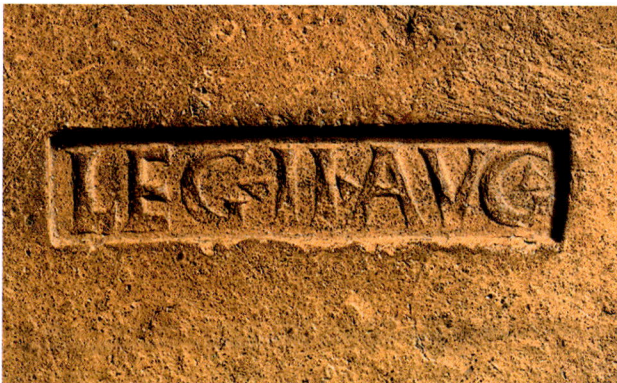

THE SECOND AUGUSTAN LEGION

Silver denarius of Augustus (27 BC – AD 14). The capricorn was the legionary badge, taken in honour of its founder Augustus (who was born when that sign was rising). (Not from Caerleon)

THE SECOND AUGUSTAN was one of thirty legions to which the security of the frontiers of the Roman Empire was entrusted. *Legio II Augusta* ('Augustus's Own') was founded by the Emperor Augustus – or reformed by him from the remnants of an existing unit, also numbered *II*. In its early days it was stationed in Spain, before being transferred to the Rhine frontier in AD 10.

It was from its German base at Strasbourg that the Second Augustan Legion was summoned in 43 to form part of the British expeditionary force. Under the command of the future emperor Vespasian, the legion conquered much of south-west Britain. From about 55, the Second Augustan occupied a fortress at Exeter, which had been designed as a permanency, with a substantial stone bath-house. There the legion remained until it was brought forward to Caerleon.

As soon as the military situation in Wales had been contained, detachments of the legion could be freed for service elsewhere in the province. From the second century onwards, the legion at *Isca*

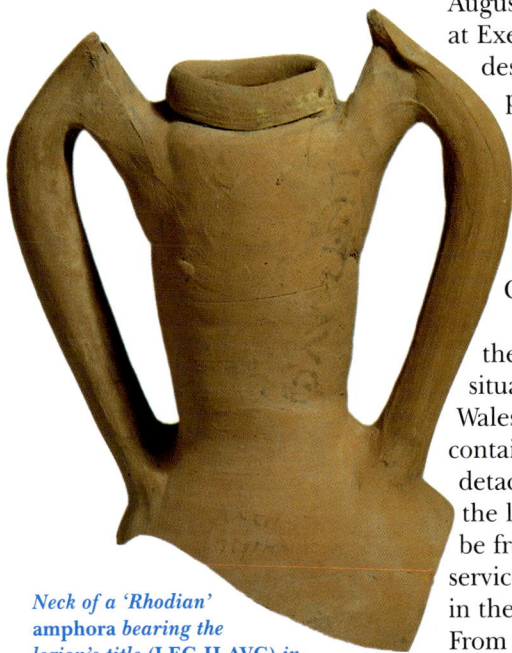

Neck of a 'Rhodian' amphora bearing the legion's title (LEG.II.AVG) in ink. Almost certainly from Crete, this type of wine jar arrived in Britain in the 50s and 60s, rarely later.

was used as a reserve of military manpower rather than a static garrison. The technical help of its specialists was in demand for military construction and engineering work, especially on the northern frontier of Britain where many building inscriptions record its presence.

Detachments were also sent to reinforce armies in other provinces, as is illustrated by a fine family tombstone from Pil-bach (p. 51), which names Tadius Exuperatus, soldier of the Second Augustan Legion, who died while on a German expedition, possibly that of the Emperor Caracalla in 213. At the end of the second century, civil war removed the legion briefly from Caerleon, when the governor of Britain, Clodius Albinus, made his bid for the throne. He crossed to Gaul with his army, and set up headquarters at Lyon, where, in February 197, he was defeated in a fierce battle by Septimius Severus. Badly mauled,

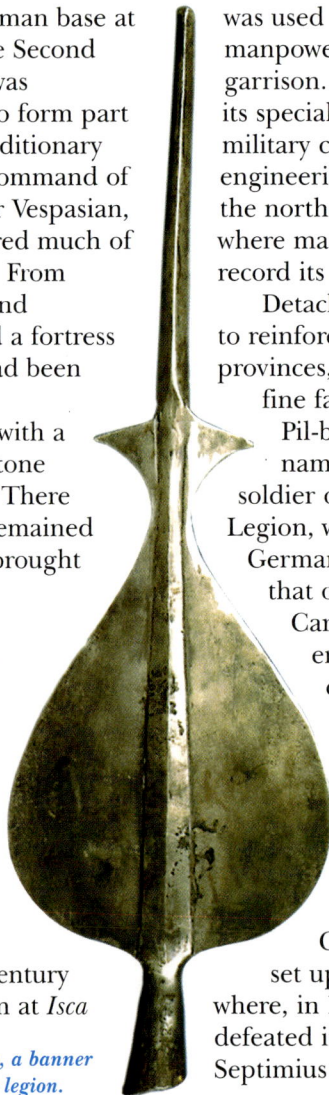

Silver tip of a vexillum, *a banner bearing the name of the legion.*

*Tombstone of Vivius Marcianus, centurion of the Second Augustan Legion, found in London. He is portrayed holding the **vitis** or vine stick, which was carried by centurions as a badge of rank, and a scroll in the other hand, perhaps reflecting his clerical duties. Marcianus was on duty in London, in the third century, when he died. (Reproduced by permission of the Museum of London)*

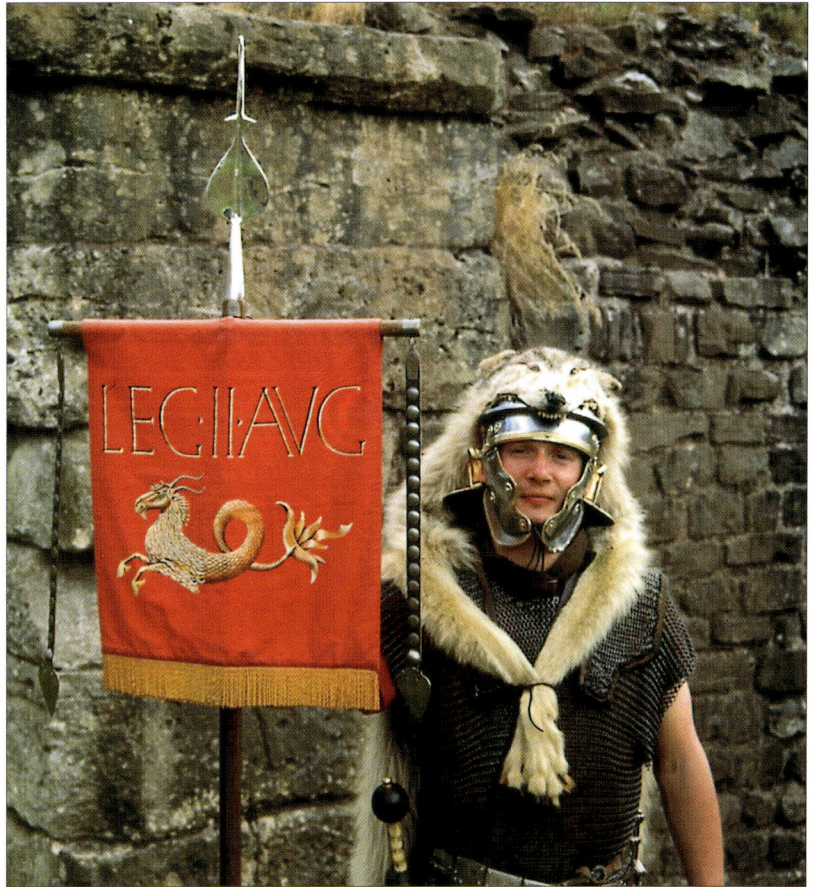

*A **vexillarius** of the Ermine Street Guard. Cohorts on detached duty followed a banner (the **vexillum**) bearing the name of their legion and its emblem, which for the Second Augustan Legion was the capricorn.*

the Second Augustan was sent back to base, presumably with replacement officers loyal to the Emperor Severus.

Detachments came and went throughout the third century. Some, however, were never to return to base, and by the middle of the century the force at Caerleon was much depleted. The troops which remained were finally withdrawn about 290. Thereafter, it is possible that part of the legion may have been stationed at the coastal fort at Cardiff, newly built in the late third century as part of a defensive system to combat the external threat of sea-borne raiders.

The late-Roman legion was very different from its earlier counterpart and was a much smaller force. By the late fourth century, an element of the legion had been moved to the fort at Richborough (Kent) to defend the south coast of Britain. This and other units traceable back to *legio II*, which had crossed to the Continent, are the last records that we have of the legion.

A PROFESSIONAL ARMY

THE LEGIONS were highly trained bodies of infantry, and formed the core of the Roman army. There were about thirty legions and these were mostly based around the perimeter of the Empire, each at its own fortress. A legion consisted of between 5,000 and 6,000 men; surprisingly the precise strength is nowhere stated in ancient sources.

A sestertius of Hadrian (117-38). The reverse shows the emperor, commander-in-chief of the army, with standard-bearers and a centurion. Disciplina symbolizes obedience to the emperor. (Not from Caerleon)

A legion was organised into ten cohorts; nine of these contained 480 men each, divided into six centuries of 80 men, while the first cohort, at the time when Caerleon was founded, consisted of about 800 men in five centuries of double-size.

The Ermine Street Guard – a society dedicated to the accurate reconstruction of Roman armour and drill – in full charge. The legions were the crack troops of the Roman army – the heavy infantry – sent out on campaigns of conquest beyond the Empire, or used to suppress rebellion within its frontier.

Attached to the legion were 120 horsemen *(equites)* who acted as scouts and dispatch riders, as well as various specialists – particularly architects and engineers – and craftsmen of all kinds.

In command of each legion was a legate *(legatus legionis)*, a man of senatorial rank, usually part-way through a graduated career of civil and military posts. The legate was assisted by six military tribunes, likewise on short-term commissions; the senior tribune, his second-in-command *(tribunus laticlavius)*, was of senatorial family, while the other five *(tribuni angusticlavii)* were drawn from the equestrian class (Roman 'knights').

The senior professional soldier was the camp prefect *(praefectus castrorum)*, who was responsible for the organisation of the fortress, training, and equipment, and took command when the legate was absent. All of these officers lived in comfortable, large houses within the fortress. Ranking below these officers were the 59 centurions, who each led a 'century' of men. These were tough experienced soldiers mostly promoted from the ranks, and hence formed the backbone of the legion. They provided the continuity of tradition essential to a disciplined fighting force.

The legionary soldier himself had to be a Roman citizen. Enlistment was voluntary, but the selection process was rigorous. A legionary was normally recruited between the age of 18 and 20, and served for a period of 25 years. During the first century AD the majority of soldiers were drawn from Italy, southern Gaul, and southern Spain; but in the course of the second century grants of Roman citizenship brought in a great influx of recruits from the provinces. A career in the army provided a young man with an ordered and secure future in an uncertain world.

THE CENTURIONS

The centurions, mostly promoted from the ranks, were tough, experienced soldiers and formed the backbone of the army. They were often brutal, and many a soldier could show scars on his back from a centurion's vine stick. The Ermine Street Guard.

THE DREAM of the ambitious legionary would have been to rise to the rank of centurion. Promotion to the centurionate was the gift of the provincial governor, and could take years; but it brought its rewards, not least in their pay, which was twenty times that of a legionary.

A centurion could easily be recognised by his armour, for he wore a shirt of mail or scale, instead of the plate-armour of the legionaries. He also wore greaves (leg guards) and a transverse-crested helmet as a sign of his rank. His sword was worn on the left and his dagger on the right, in opposite fashion to the legionary.

Centurions also carried a vine-stick *(vitis)*, both as a symbol of authority and to use in their disciplinary role. As today, military decorations were awarded for valour in battle: such as a pair of silver *torques* (Celtic neck-rings), or a set of silvered medals *(phalerae)* attached to a harness fitting over his armoured shirt.

A centurion might spend his whole career – and some completed over 40 years' service – in the same legion, but others served in a number of legions. The five centurions of the first cohort outranked all the others, and were themselves a hierarchy; the chief centurion was known as the *primus pilus* ('first spear'), a rank held for one year either before retirement or further promotion – in the army or to administrative posts outside it.

THE STANDARDS

A centurial standard-bearer (signifer) wearing a shirt of small brass scales, sewn to a linen undergarment, and a bear-skin. The standard (signum) takes the form of a spear-shaft decorated with a number of silvered medallions and is topped by the sign of a hand, as a reminder to the soldiers of the gesture of loyalty which they made at their oath-taking. The standard, equipment and dress, reconstructed here, are based on scenes from Trajan's Column and figured tombstones. The Ermine Street Guard.

THE STANDARDS embodied the very 'souls' of the legion and its units, and were revered by the men and fiercely protected. A legion had three main types of standard. The eagle (aquila) was the standard of the legion as a whole, and during the Empire it was made of gold.

The legion also carried a standard bearing the image of the emperor (imago), which served to identify him to his troops, and to focus their loyalty on him. Both the aquila and the imago were entrusted to the safe-keeping of the first cohort. Each century had its own individual standard (signum), borne by a signifer.

There were also banners (vexilla), bearing the legion's title and badge, and others for detachments serving away from the camp. In peacetime, the legion's standards were kept in the 'chapel of the standards' at the headquarters, and their worship formed an important element in the official religion.

To carry any of these sacred standards was a mark of special honour. Standard-bearers normally wore shirts of mail or scale armour and, as a mark of status, they were adorned with the skins of wolves or bears. They also held responsibility for the safekeeping of soldiers' pay and savings. The eagle-carrier (aquilifer) was responsible for the legionary pay-chest, which

The gravestone of Gaius Valerius Victor, a standard-bearer in the Second Augustan Legion. His original home was Lyon in southern Gaul. (On loan from the British Museum)

D(is) M(anibus) / G(aius) Valerius / G(ai) f(ilius) / Galeria (tribu) Victor / Lugduni sig(nifer) leg(ionis) II Aug(ustae) / stip(endiorum) XVII annor(um) XLV cu/ra(m) agent(e) Annio Perpetuo h(erede)

'To the spirits of the departed; Gaius Valerius Victor, son of Gaius, of the Galerian voting-tribe, from Lugdunum, standard-bearer of the Second Augustan Legion, of 17 years' service, aged 45, set up under the charge of Annius Perpetuus, his heir.'

was held for security in the 'chapel of the standards'.

The centurial standard-bearer (*signifer*) was one of three junior officers in a century. He

A horn-blower (cornicen). *A blast on the horn (cornu) drew the soldiers' attention to their standard. The Ermine Street Guard.*

would have been a man of good character and education, who had to enjoy the trust of the men. As the officer responsible for the men's savings, his paperwork included issuing receipts for deposits and preparing detailed accounts.

In battle, the tall centurial-standards served as rallying points for the men. Loud blasts on a horn (*cornu*) would draw attention to the standard which, with movements, could be used to convey simple commands.

THE LEGIONARY AND HIS EQUIPMENT

ON ENLISTMENT, a recruit was given a posting to the legion in which he would serve. On arrival in the camp, he and his fellow recruits took an oath of loyalty to the emperor, and began their basic training. Legionaries were expected to be very fit and their regular exercise included running, jumping and swimming across rivers.

Soldiers attended weapons drill every morning – and twice daily for new recruits. They trained against wooden stakes using dummy swords and javelins made of wood and wickerwork shields, which were double the normal weight to improve their strength. Soldiers were also trained in basic horse-manship, the use of the bow and sling-shot. On the parade ground, the legionary was taught to march in step and to obey instinctively the orders of his centurion. Field exercises were strenuous, including long route marches carrying heavy packs, practice in the construction of temporary camps and battle manoeuvres.

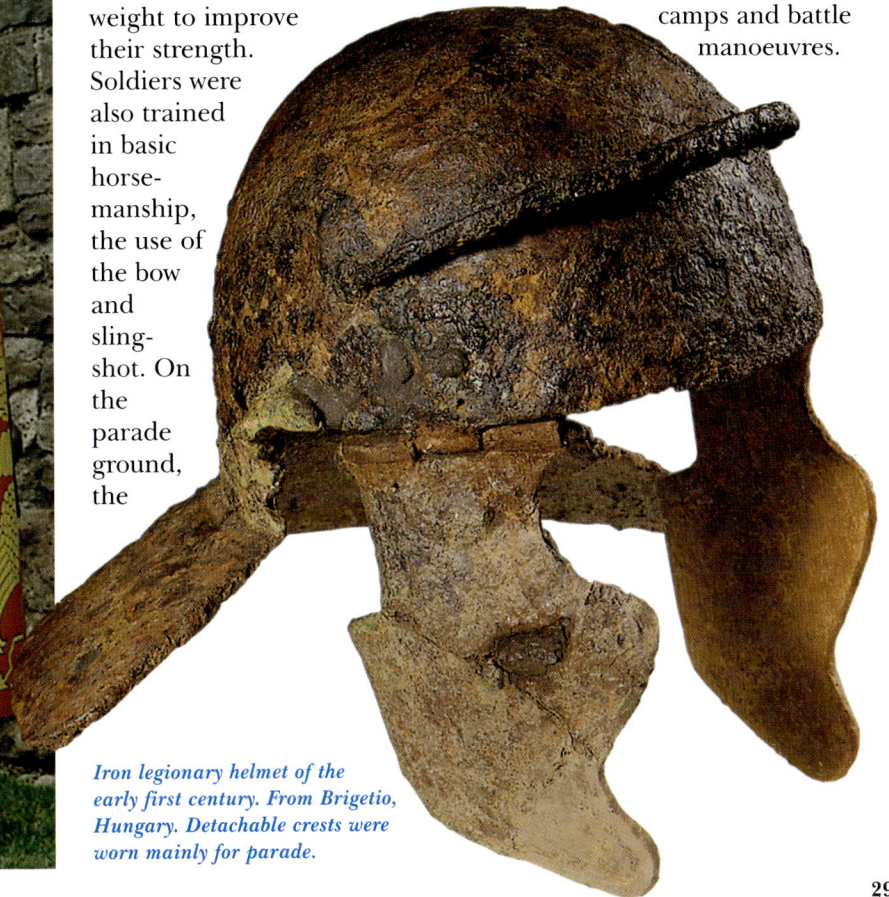

Iron legionary helmet of the early first century. From Brigetio, Hungary. Detachable crests were worn mainly for parade.

Our knowledge of Roman military equipment is derived partly through illustrations on stone, such as Trajan's Column and figured gravestones, and partly from surviving pieces. The basic legionary issue was largely standardised.

Hinge-fitting, buckle and tie-loops from suits of flexible plate armour (lorica segmentata) *and copper alloy hangers from the leather apron-straps worn to protect the lower abdomen. On the whole, only small scraps of military equipment are found at Caerleon, for the legion would have removed all weapons and armour upon departure from the fortress.*

Each soldier carried two javelins (*pila*) which would be thrown at the beginning of an engagement to disable as many of the enemy as possible. Over 2 m in length, the *pilum* was designed with a long untempered shank, which bent upon impact so that the enemy could not immediately throw it back.

The short, thrusting sword (*gladius*) – an effective weapon in close combat – was suspended from a shoulder-belt on the right side so that it could be drawn underarm with the right hand while the left held up the large heavy shield. A dagger (*pugio*) was attached to his waist-belt on the left side, but this item seems to have disappeared from legionary equipment by the beginning of the second century.

For protection the legionary wore an iron or brass helmet with a reinforcement at the front, hinged cheek-pieces and wide neck-guard (with carrying handle). A soldier of the later first and second centuries would have worn flexible body armour (*lorica segmentata*), consisting of overlapping segments of thin iron sheet held together by vertical leather straps internally,

Bone and copper alloy chapes, which covered the points of scabbards.

hinges and buckles at the shoulder and chest, and laces down the front and back. An apron of leather straps with riveted metal discs was suspended from the belt to protect the lower abdomen. For further defence, the legionary carried a large rectangular shield (*scutum*), made of laminated strips of wood covered in linen and hide; the edge was reinforced with bronze binding and the hand grip was protected by a metal boss. The front of the shield was elaborately painted.

Weapons and armour were subject to tight controls and, although paid for by the individual soldiers when issued from the stores, had to be surrendered on discharge – a measure to prevent equipment falling into the wrong hands. The cost of repairs and replacements were met by stoppages from pay – always the best encouragement for a soldier to take good care of his equipment.

A group of iron weapons of the third century AD: spearheads; pilum-head; arrowhead.

A leaden bread-stamp, reading 'Century of Quintinius Aquila'. Each century baked its own bread, and sometimes marked it. The unleavened loaf was baked recently.

THE LIFE
OF A LEGIONARY

MUCH of a soldier's service was probably spent in peaceful conditions. Training and exercise were therefore essential to keep the troops fully prepared for fighting and to avoid the dangers of boredom.

For the non-specialist, some duties were strictly military – as sentries at headquarters, as road patrols and escorts, or on detached service. But many were mundane chores connected with the running of the camp: cleaning the latrines, stoking furnaces at the baths, or sweeping out the barracks.

Other occupations included the construction and maintenance of buildings and roads, an involvement in mining, farming, and the manufacture of a long list of items such as arms, armour, tiles, bricks and so on. Hence, a legion needed numerous specialists: as well as the building craftsmen, there were farriers, arrowsmiths, coppersmiths, helmet-makers, wagon-makers, swordcutlers, bow-makers, butchers, clerks and

A locally-made money-pot, second century AD. The scatter of coins is part of a hoard of savings of about AD 180, found in a centurion's quarters.

(193-211) perhaps to 450 *denarii*. Mounting monetary inflation led to further increases, first by Caracalla (211-17) to 675 *denarii*, but thereafter, as the real value of pay decreased, a greater dependence was placed upon payment in kind. Legionaries also received large monetary awards (donatives), probably paid in gold coins, after a victory, or on the accession of a new emperor. Stoppages were made from the legionary's basic pay for rations, clothing, equipment, the burial club, and the regimental dinner. After compulsory savings had been deducted as well, the soldier may have received no more than pocket-money.

The soldiers' diet was ample and varied. The staple foods were wheat – which could be made into bread, porridge or pasta – pork, cheese, salt and sour wine. These were supplemented by a wide range of vegetables (lentils, beans, cabbage, carrots and celery), fruits (apples, pears, plums, strawberries and raspberries), and animal products (mutton, lamb, beef, venison, hare, fowl and fish).

Imported luxuries included figs, dates and olives. Wine was brought in *amphorae* from Italy and Spain, and wooden barrels from Gaul. From Spain also came olive oil, and the fish-sauce

doctors. Legionaries with these skills were known as *immunes*, and were excused from routine fatigues.

A surviving duty-roster from Egypt, for ten days in October 87, reveals a varied existence for an ordinary legionary. One of the men listed worked in the armoury, the quarries, the baths and on the artillery, as well as doing other general duties on different days over that period.

In over two hundred years legionary pay was increased only twice; from the time of Julius Caesar onwards the rate was 225 silver *denarii* per annum, raised by Domitian (81-96) to 300 *denarii*, and by Septimius Severus

Pottery inkwell, an iron stylus for writing on waxed tablets, a seal-box and a lead property marker inscribed 'Century of Vibius Proculus'. The legion kept meticulous records – military reports, rosters, lists of supplies and requests for leave – and soldiers wrote letters to their families and friends. Many documents and letters have been found at the Roman fort of **Vindolanda**, south of Hadrian's Wall.

Soldiers were not permitted to marry during service, and so found relationships with local women, raising families with sons destined for the army in their turn. Eventually the ban was lifted by Severus at the close of the second century AD.

Off-duty soldiers may have visited the Fortress Baths, which served not only as a place for washing, but also, as finds show, a leisure and social centre. As well as the halls and pools of varying temperatures, there was ample provision at the baths for exercise, games and swimming too in the outdoor pool. Snacks and drinks were on sale here, and time could be spent gambling and playing board games.

On the many festival days, entertainment, in the form of blood-sports and gladiatorial combat, was provided in the Amphitheatre.

A soldier would also have longed for leave – to sleep, to visit friends and family, to tend to his financial affairs or to squander his money on women, drink and gambling. A bribe to the centurion often assisted the application.

Iron padlock and keys for tumbler and rotary locks. A variety of locks were used to secure doors and chests.

(garum) used in many Roman recipes. With no centralised mess at the fortress, the men probably ate in their quarters, preparing their meals in ovens set behind the defences and in the cookhouses which were eventually built outside most turrets.

BARRACKS

Capricorn Centre. The front room was used by the men for storing their equipment.

THE BARRACK-BLOCKS, one for each century, took up a large part of the fortress. The blocks, which vary very little from one fortress to another, are long, narrow L-shaped buildings. Those that can be seen at Caerleon (Prysg Field) have twelve pairs of rooms fronted by a verandah, while at the wider end is a larger suite of rooms housing the centurion.

Each century was divided into ten mess-units (*contubernia*), each of eight men, who shared a pair of rooms in the barracks, or a tent on campaign. In theory, only ten pairs of rooms should be needed for the 80 men in the century, but there are often extra rooms and these were probably needed for storage, or new recruits, or the junior officers. The soldiers of each *contubernium* used the smaller, outer room for storing their personal kit and equipment and the inner, slightly larger, one for sleeping.

The centurion's quarters are spacious and more elaborate, with a range of rooms opening off a central corridor. Some of these were for his personal use and included a latrine and washroom, but the century's office and record-room would also be located here.

The reconstructed barrack-rooms in the Capricorn Centre are very similar in size to those that are visible in the Prysg Field barracks. Our knowledge of the sleeping arrangements and the appearance of the barrack-rooms is limited, for only the floors and lowest levels of walls are usually found. Everything above ground level is a matter of opinion. The rooms would have been less crammed than it might appear, however, for it is likely that some of the eight men would have been on duty elsewhere within the fortress at any one time.

Capricorn Centre; the inner room. The sleeping arrangements are unknown. The legionaries may have slept on mattresses on the floor, on beds or bunks. Bunks seem the most likely option, for they would have saved space. The room has a fireplace for winter heating.

SUPPLY

THE PROVISIONING of a legion would have been a considerable task. A wide range of items was required – food and cooking implements, clothing, arms and armour, tents, animals, building materials and so on – demanding products in both raw and finished states.

The long list of skilled craftsmen engaged in the production of goods indicates that the legion was self-sufficient to a great extent. Some worked in the construction-shops (*fabricae*) within the fortress, where there are extensive traces of metalworking debris, no doubt resulting from the manufacture and maintenance of equipment. Some civilians may also have been employed in the workshops.

The soldiers also won the raw materials themselves and iron, lead, coal, timber and building-stones were to be found at no great distance from *Isca*. The Roman state held the most valuable mineral rights, and also kept control, on behalf of the legion, of various holdings essential for supply, such as the brickworks and tilery, limekilns, quarries and so on. An area of pastureland (*prata*) was also maintained to graze the

Severn, were used for such a purpose. Here the legion was actively involved in the careful drainage and reclamation of these excellent grasslands.

Adequate supplies of grain were always held in store at the fortress. In the early years after the conquest much of the grain required had to be transported from the south-east of Britain, while some was even imported from the Mediterranean.

Leather was used for a wide variety of goods: tents, shoes, shield-covers, bags, kit, harness etc. Huge quantities of sheep- or goat-skins, calf-skins and ox-hides were needed, and the pastoral farmers of Wales would have been among the main

mounts, draught-animals, and the dairy or store cattle.

There is little doubt but that the Gwent levels, fringing the

Samian vessels.
In the first century, most samian came from south Gaul, but by the second century, the central Gaulish factories took over as the main source.

Samian bowl, by Germanus of south Gaul, about AD 65-75. Decorated with a stylized hunting scene with hounds chasing hares into nets, all within a vineyard. Bowls with relief patterns were made in moulds.

A range of black burnished ware vessels from Dorset; ranging in date from first to fourth centuries AD.

suppliers to the Roman army. Unlike leather, which is only rarely preserved, pottery is found in abundance. Both tablewares and cooking vessels were in constant demand, and most were cheap to make and easily replaced when broken.

Some pottery was made at Caerleon, at first by legionary craftsmen, but later by civilians. Much more pottery, such as black burnished ware cooking-pots from Dorset, came from the many establishments in Britain.

Caerleon ware: a flagon, field flask, **mortarium** *rim inscribed with the owner's name –* **VALERIUS MARTIALIS** *– jug-neck waster and a mould for an oil lamp. In the first and second centuries AD pottery was made close to the fortress, originally by legionary craftsmen and later by civilians.*

More attractive was the fine glossy red samian ware – mainly bowls, plates and cups – which was imported in large quantities into the province from Gaul in the first and second centuries AD.

Other imports include such items as fine glassware, mainly from northern Gaul and the Rhineland but also from the Eastern Mediterranean, and bronzes and pottery lamps from Gaul.

Mould-blown bottle. First or second century AD.

RELIGION AND SUPERSTITION

RELIGION had a powerful influence on the soldier's life. Soldiers naturally fought better if they knew that the gods were on their side and before all campaigns, the omens were studied, sacrifices were offered and vows undertaken. While units were stationed at their permanent headquarters there was a regular calendar of festivals to be observed.

A Bath stone relief of Fortuna and Bonus Eventus, set up by Cornelius Castus and Iulia Belismicus, his wife, in the baths outside the east corner of the fortress. Fortuna was the recipient of numerous dedications in bath-houses, for it was believed that when man was naked, he was particularly vulnerable to malignant forces and needed protection.

A copy of a Roman military calendar of festivals, from Dura Europos on the river Euphrates, demonstrates the emphasis which was placed on the most ancient and traditional deities – Jupiter, Juno, Minerva, Mars, Neptune, Victory and Roma – and on imperial anniversaries.

The veneration of the emperor and his ancestors was an important element in this official religion, and was a means of upholding his imperial authority. Another significant ingredient in the religious life of the legion was the worship of the standards, a unifying element in all the diverse beliefs. The legionary eagle *(aquila)* was closely associated with Jupiter, the highest and most powerful in the Roman pantheon of gods. The shrine of the standards *(aedes)*, which would also have contained statues of the emperor and perhaps figures of deities, was situated in the headquarters at the centre of the fortress.

Inscription recording the restoration of the Temple of Diana by the legionary legate, about 250; Postumius Varus went on to become Prefect of Rome in 271, under Aurelian. The site of the temple, outside the fortress, has yet to be located.

T(itus) Fl(avius) Postumius / [V]arus v(ir) c(larissimus) leg(atus) / templ(um) Dianae / restituit

'Titus Flavius Postumius Varus, senator and legate (of the legion), restored the temple of Diana.'

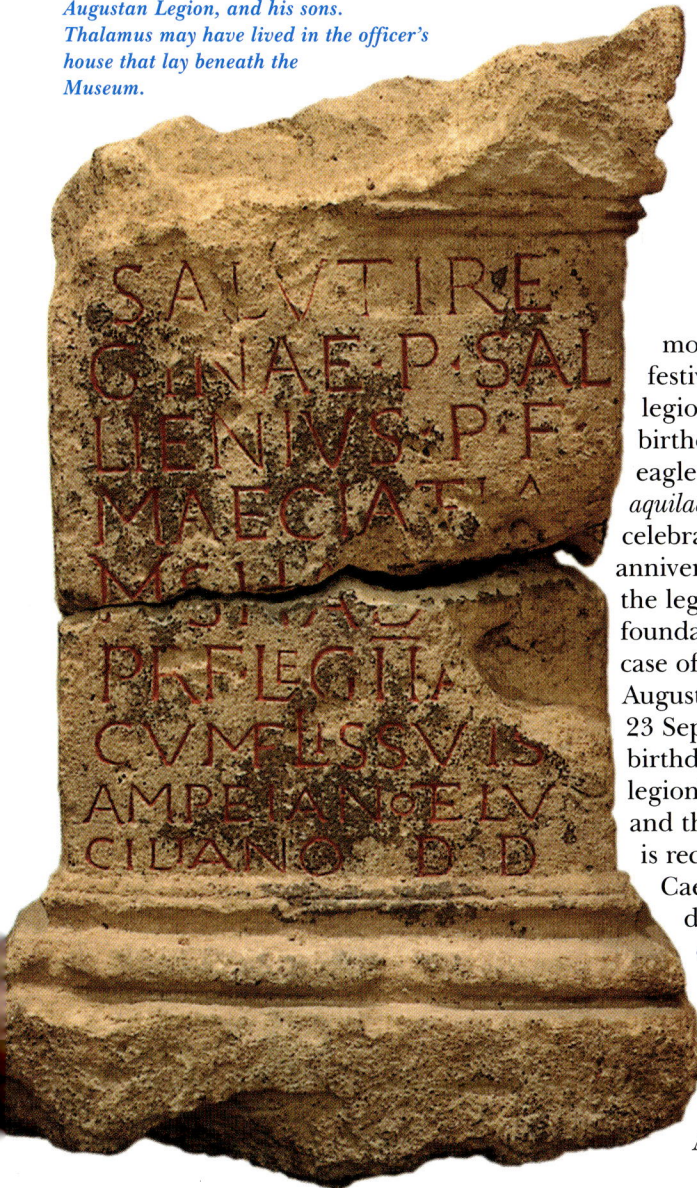

A small copper alloy ram, a symbol of fertility normally associated with Mercury.

One of the most important festivals in a legion was the birthday of the eagle *(natalis aquilae)*, which celebrated the anniversary of the legion's foundation. In the case of the Second Augustan this was 23 September (the birthday of the legion's founder), and the anniversary is recorded at Caerleon in two dedications, dating to 234 and 244, both made by the chief centurions of the time. Also of special military significance were the *Rosaliae Signorum* held on two days in May, when the standards were paraded garlanded with roses.

The official religion, associated with the *aedes* and parade-ground, only partly met a man's needs. Each soldier would have worshipped his own gods, perhaps a favourite classical deity – Mars was very popular in military cults; but a clerk, for example, may have chosen Minerva, the goddess of writing and learning. Soldiers also honoured local deities, either brought with them from their homelands or adopted from the area in which the legion was based.

The Romans were very superstitious and used charms and amulets to bring luck and ward off evil. Some gods were depicted on everyday objects to provide protection.

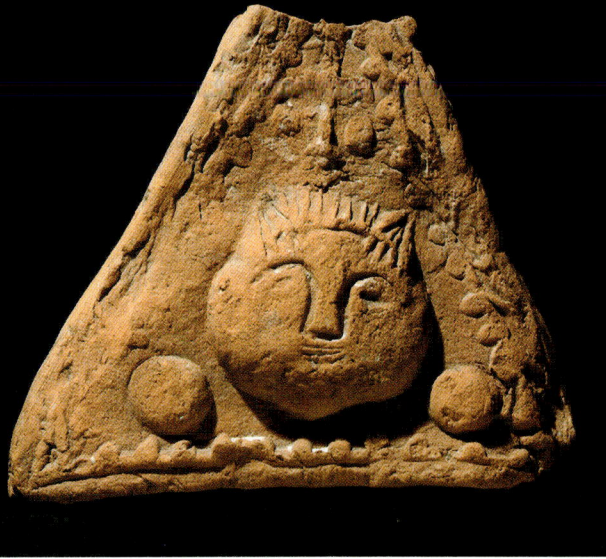

*Ornamental gable-tiles (antefixa) manufactured in the legionary tilery. They bear protective and evil-averting emblems.
(above) Gorgon's head, thought to attract evil and so deflect it from the occupants of the building.
(right) Head, possibly of Venus, ancestress of Augustus and so protectress of the legion.*

Gem engraved with the god Mercury. Shown holding the herald's wand with a head of entwined snakes (caduceus) and a moneybag, which are his attributes. As the god of wealth he was a very popular charm.

Some of the eastern religions were to prove especially popular with soldiers, and at Caerleon inscriptions attest temples, sited outside the fortress, of Mithras (a god of Persian origin) and Jupiter Dolichenus (a Syrian cult).

Mithraism, open only to men, was organised as a secret society and involved seven grades of initiation. Mithras struggled, ever-victorious, with the powers of evil on man's behalf, and like all mystery cults initiates were promised a happy life after death. Mithraism was exceptional in that it insisted on a high moral code, with the emphasis of honesty, purity and courage.

These mystery cults provided a sharp contrast with the more formalized and impersonal religions of the Roman state.

ROMAN GEMS

The goddess Roma. Cornelian. Second century AD. Symbolising in human form the city of Rome.

A SPLENDID collection of 88 engraved gemstones of first to early third century date was found during the excavation of the Fortress Baths. Most of this remarkable collection – one of the largest single deposits to be found anywhere in the Roman Empire – was retrieved from the sediments of a large drain beneath the cold hall of the baths.

The Fortress Baths gems were lost during the period AD 80 and 230 – and so at a rate of less than one a year. The gemstones would originally have been set in finger-rings, and served as signets and as charms or talismans for their owners. They were the product of extremely skilled craftsmen who worked on a minute scale without the aid of magnification.

The gems are engraved with a wide array of deities, personifications and symbols. A range of semi-precious stones, mostly varieties of quartz, was used for engraving. Most of the Caerleon stones were probably brought from far afield: Cyprus, Egypt, India and Ceylon provided much of the raw material for the Roman gem-cutting centres. At the lowest end of the market, cheap gems were made simply by casting coloured glass paste in a mould.

The Fortress Baths gems were lost during the period between AD 80 and 230. Most of the 88 gems from the Fortress Baths belonged to legionary soldiers, but some may have been lost by the civilians and women who were also admitted to the baths.

Crescent Moon and Stars. Citrine. Second or third century AD. These astrological symbols suggest the notion of eternity.

The warrior-goddess Minerva. Nicolo. First century AD. Minerva was protectress of soldiers and had powers of healing.

Eagle devouring a hare. Red Jasper. Second or third century AD. The imagery is military; the eagle, signifying the imperial legions, is all powerful and vanquishes all before it.

CIVILIAN SETTLEMENTS

THE CAMP followers would have arrived soon after the legion established its base at Caerleon. There would have been merchants, shopkeepers, craftsmen, girlfriends and all the others who depended on the army for their existence.

Many women adopted provincial Roman dress as here. But the great majority of the population were peasants and they retained their language, their habits and customs, and continued to worship their old gods. (Geoff Wills)

The fortress and associated civilian settlements.

At first, they would have set up makeshift stalls and tents, but in time these would have been replaced by permanent buildings and the *canabae* was born. Also, it would not have taken long for the native population to recognize the requirements of the army as an opportunity for personal enrichment.

Legionaries would have spent much of their off-duty time in the civil settlement outside the fortress. Soldiers could find entertainment of all kinds – taverns, snack bars, shops – or attend to personal worship at the temples of their many gods. Three temples are known from inscriptions – to Diana, Jupiter Dolichenus and Mithras – but remain unlocated within the civilian suburbs.

The civilian settlement lay on three sides of the fortress. On the south-west, a walled parade-ground was sited north-west of the street leading down to the wharves; to the south-east lay the Ampitheatre. Beyond these structures, towards the river, came the buildings of the civil settlement, including a large market-hall *(macellum)*. Of domestic buildings there are few signs: a close group of six houses or shops lying at an

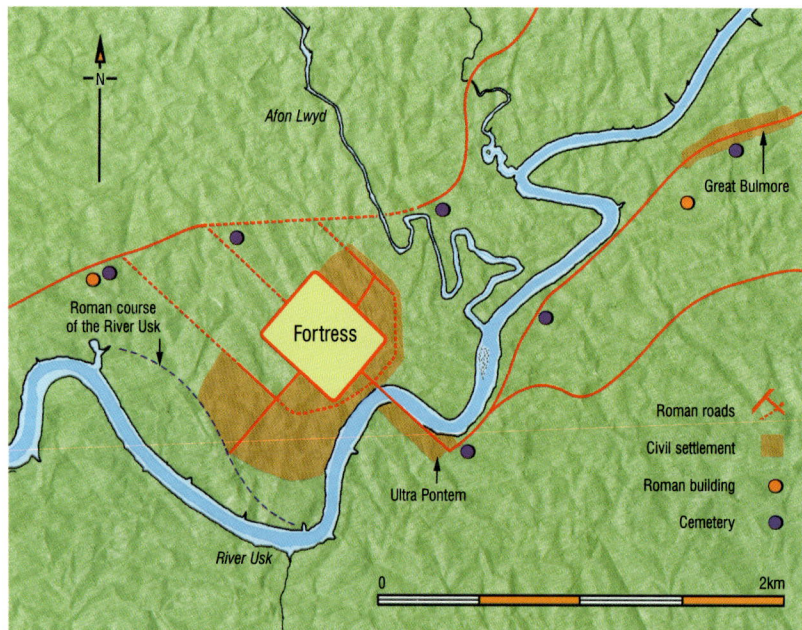

Head of a bone hairpin, carved in the form of a female bust. First century AD. Some elaborate hairstyles worn by women required many pins.

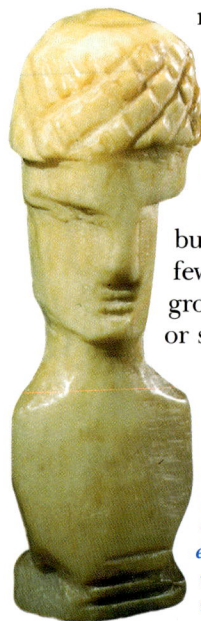

Afon Lwyd

Great Bulmore

Roman course of the River Usk

Fortress

Ultra Pontem

River Usk

Roman roads
Civil settlement
Roman building
Cemetery

0   2km

angle to the bypass road, a large square building with central courtyard, and a few others quite widely spaced are the only buildings yet to be excavated. To the north-east of the fortress, extensive excavations have uncovered twenty-two buildings, ranging from 'cottages' with two or three rooms, to strip-buildings (workshops) and larger structures. Some were associated with small-scale agriculture on reclaimed marshland bordering the Afon Lwyd, and others produced evidence for craft activity, especially iron-smelting.

On the southern approaches to the Usk bridge traces of further buildings have been recovered. A bath-house between the east corner and the south-east gate – the 'Castle' baths, so called because it lay within the grounds of the medieval castle – probably formed part of the *canabae*. However, there is

Tweezers, forceps and ear-pick or ointment scoop. Personal hygiene of the inhabitants of the civil settlement is reflected by the many toiletry items found there.

45

A gold ear-ring; a garnet drop ear-ring and part of a gold necklet.

Bone and copper alloy needles. The fine copper alloy needle would have been used for sewing or darning, while the larger ones were probably sacking needles. Also shown are two weaving tablets used for making braid belts.

Candlestick, an alternative to the oil lamp. Manufactured locally in the second century AD.

evidence that the women and children from the civilian settlement were, at times, allowed to use the Fortress Baths, to judge from the hair-pins, scraps of jewellery and even one or two milk teeth lost there.

Further afield at Great Bulmore, 2 km to the east of the fortress on the left bank of the Usk, lay an extensive roadside settlement. Here, some thirteen strip-buildings have been identified so far – some of which have produced evidence of metalworking and glass making – but other structures are known to exist. The inhabitants would no doubt have had close links with the fortress, providing services and goods to the legion.

Caerwent (*Venta Silurum*), the capital of the Silures, was in easy travelling distance of Caerleon, and the legionary soldiers would have spent some of their leisure time in the shops and inns of the town. The proximity of Caerwent and the commitments which took detachments of the legion to northern Britain and elsewhere appears to have prevented the development of a full township outside the fortress, as seen at York for example.

DEATH
AND BURIAL

A SOLDIER was assured a decent funeral, for every man was a member of a burial club, financed by compulsory deductions from his pay. There are extensive cemeteries in the vicinity of the fortress.

Until the end of the second century most bodies were cremated, and the burnt bones were usually interred in a pot, or sometimes in an *amphora* or a glass bottle. By far the most interesting of the cremations from Caerleon is the 'pipe-burial' found in 1927 at the foot of the hillside to the south-east of the fortress. The cylindrical leaden canister, buried in a stone-lined pit, contained the cremated bones of a man aged at least 35, wrapped in a linen cloth.

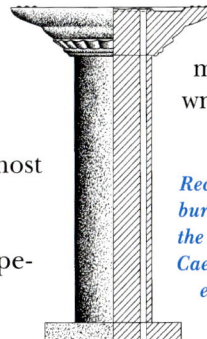

Reconstruction of the leaden 'pipe-burial.' The funerary table above the grave is based on a lost Caerleon piece recorded in the eighteenth century.

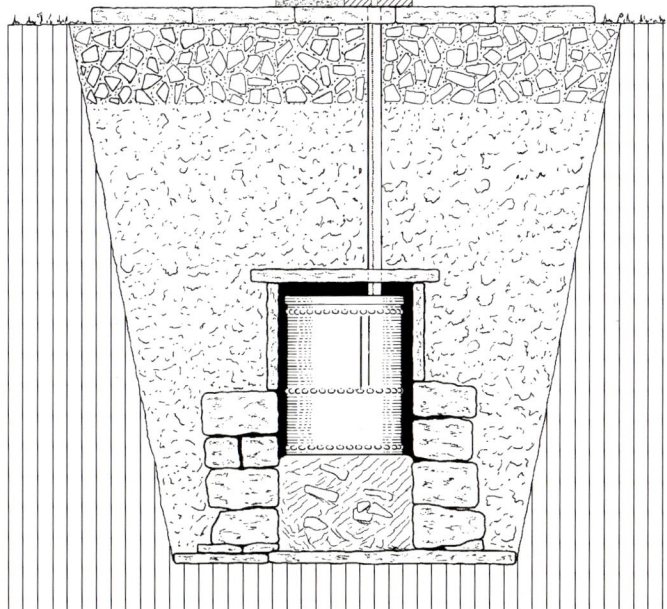

Ivory carving, probably from a burial, in the form of a tragic mask.

0   100 cm

Glass bottle containing cremated bones, found in 1847 in the cemetery to the north-east of the fortress. By far the greater number of burials in the legionary cemeteries are cremations, and range in date from the first to the end of the second century.

Inserted in the lid was a leaden pipe down which libations of wine, milk and honey would have been poured from the surface.

More recent excavations suggest that the burial lay within an elaborate, circular structure. Anatomical analysis of thirteen cremations excavated at the surrounding cemetery show that all but one were female, mostly below the age of thirty.

The third century saw a change to inhumation as the dominant rite, and a leaden and several rough Bath stone coffins are recorded from the legionary cemeteries. Traces of wooden coffins have also been found in four slab-lined graves at the native settlement of Great Bulmore.

Grave-goods accompany some of the burials, but are generally meagre, usually consisting of a simple

The upper half of a Bath stone funerary sculpture from Little Bulmore. It shows a bearded man with his right hand on the shoulder of his son. The lettering in the gable was probably carved in the eighteenth century.

Aurelius Herculanus

Gravestone of Aurelius Herculanus, from a cemetery to the north-east of the fortress. Herculanus was one of the 120 horsemen (equites) attached to the legion as scouts and dispatch riders.

D(is) M(anibus) / Aurelius Hercula/nus aeques vixit an/nos XXVIII coniux f/aciendum curavi/t

'To the spirits of the departed; Aurelius Herculanus, horseman, lived 28 years; his wife had this set up.'

offering-vessel – such as a dish, jar or glass perfume-bottle – or less frequently a coin, the so-called 'ferryman's fee'. Most interesting are two small ivory plaques, both of which have been adapted, perhaps as ornaments for a lady's work-box.

In the case of important burials a tomb was probably erected, perhaps even taking the form of a

small building, where various rituals to commemorate the dead could be conducted. Tessellated pavements recorded at St Julian's and Pil-bach most probably belonged to such places. The majority of burials were probably marked by monuments, of which the most imposing to survive is the upper half of a Bath stone sculpture from Little Bulmore. Over thirty inscribed gravestones have also come to light. Those of tablet-like form must have been attached to the masonry of tombs, but others with the inscription towards the top of the slab would have

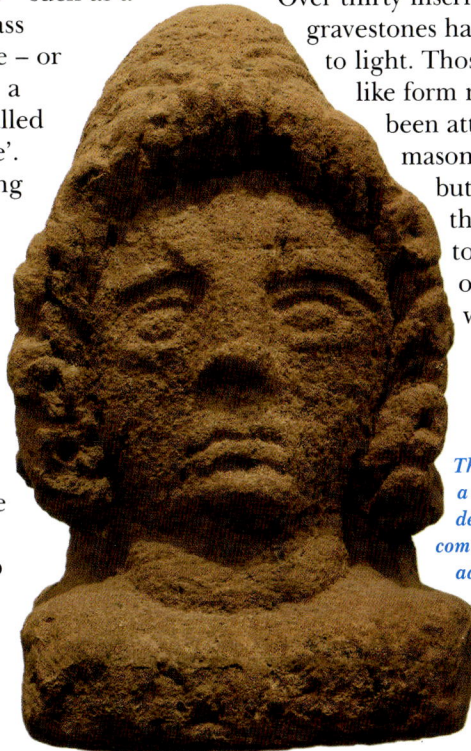

This head of Attis – a symbol of both death and life-to-come – would have adorned a masonry tomb. It was found within the cemetery area to the west of the fortress.

Titus Flavius Candidus

Memorial to a legionary soldier, found at Little Bulmore. Candidus' home town of **Ulpia Traiana** *is the present-day Xanten on the Rhine, in Germany.*

D(is) M(anibus) / T(itus) Flavius Candi/dus Ulp(ia) Traiana / m(iles) leg(ionis) II Aug(ustae) / sti(pendiorum) VII an(norum) XXVII / fra(ter) c(uravit)

'To the spirits of the departed; Titus Flavius Candidus, from Ulpia Traiana, soldier of the Second Augustan Legion, of 7 years' service, aged 27, his brother had this set up.'

individuals they commemorate and the organisation of the Roman army. Funerary inscriptions tend to have a similar format, and use standard abbreviations. The epitaph was usually introduced by the formula *D(is) M(anibus)* – 'to the spirits of the departed' – which hallowed the monument. This was followed by personal details, which if given in full would include the name of the

been set deeply into the ground, like the free-standing gravestones of today.

Military gravestones provide an important source of information, both about the

Julius Valens

On retirement from the legion, Julius Valens, like many other veterans who had formed attachments with local women, started a new life close to the fortress. He allegedly survived to become a centenarian, while his wife Secundina, who is commemorated on a separate stone, died at the age of 75. The two memorials were found together with six others at Great Bulmore in c 1815, in a small rectangular building – not a mausoleum as once thought but a dwelling paved with re-used gravestones.

[D(is) M(anibus)] / Iul(ius) Valens vet(eranus) / leg(ionis) II Aug(ustae) vixit / annis C Iul(ia) / Secundina coniunx / et Iul(ius) Martinus filius / f(aciendum) c(uraverunt)

'To the spirits of the departed; Julius Valens, veteran of the Second Augustan Legion, lived 100 years; Julia Secundina, his wife, and Julius Martinus, his son, had this set up.'

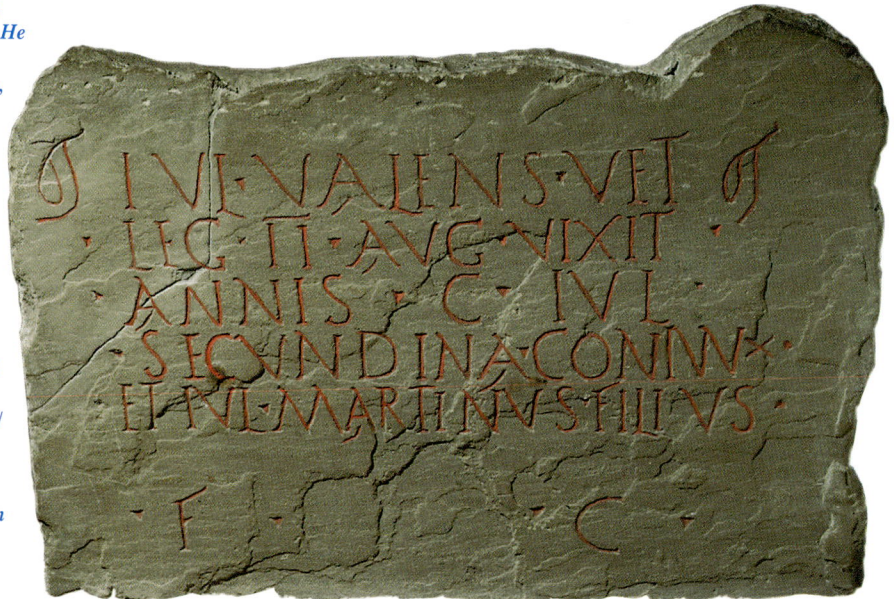

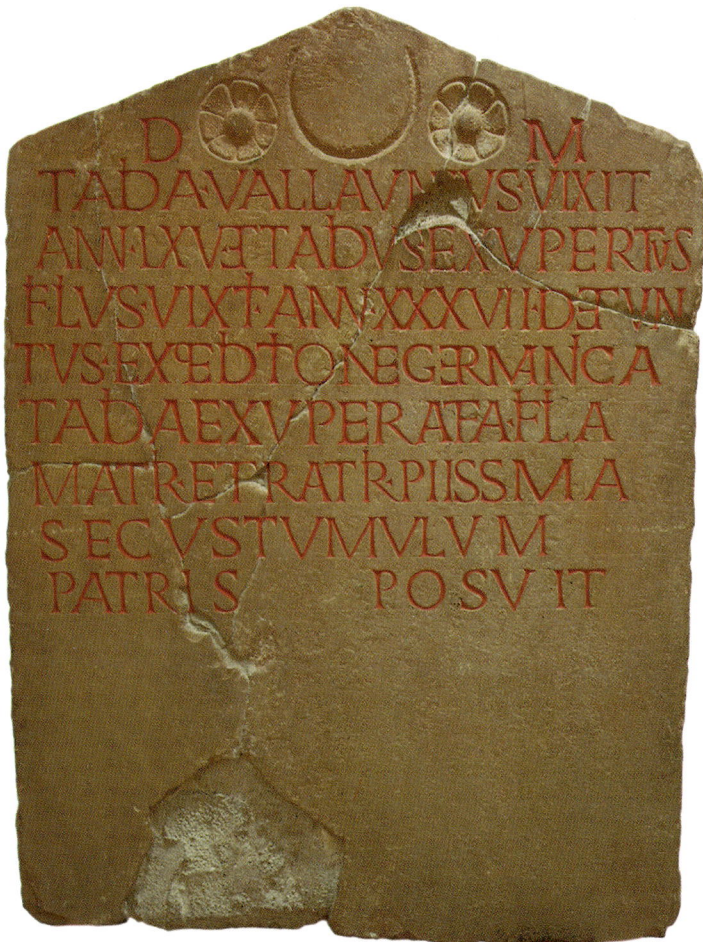

deceased, his father's name, his voting tribe and birthplace, as well as his rank, age and length of service. In addition, the text was usually closed with the name of the heir who was responsible for having the monument erected.

Of those soldiers which are recorded on gravestones from Caerleon, three died in their later twenties, five in the decade 35-45, and three at over 60, including one at 100! A wider survey reveals that about half of those who joined up at 18 survived to retirement in their forties. There are also a number of gravestones commemorating women from the Caerleon cemeteries.

ROMAN BRITAIN

Map of Roman Britain showing legionary fortresses, frontiers, principal towns and main roads.

Inchtuthil

ANTONINE WALL

HADRIAN'S WALL

Military:	Permanent legionary fortress
	Legionary fortress evacuated
Civil:	Colonia
	Tribal capital
	Other towns

York

Lincoln

Chester

Wroxeter

Colchester

Carmarthen

Gloucester

Usk

Cirencester

Verulamium

Caerleon

Caerwent

London

Bath

Exeter

NATIONAL MUSEUMS & GALLERIES OF WALES

CREATION

Genesis 1:1 – 2:3

STORIES OF THE
BIBLE

Illustrations by
Gustavo Mazali

scandinavia

STORIES OF THE BIBLE
Copyright © 2004 Scandinavia Publishing House
Drejervej 15,3 DK-2400 Copenhagen NV, Denmark
Tel.: (+45) 3531 0330   Fax: (+45) 3531 0334
E-mail: info@scanpublishing.dk
Website: www.scanpublishing.dk
Illustration copyright © Gustavo Mazali
Design by Ben Alex
Printed in China
Hardcover ISBN 87 7247 783 0
Softcover ISBN 87 7247 784 9

The beginning

In the beginning there was nothing—except for God.

God said, "Let there be light!"
—and suddenly there was light all over.

Then God made the earth—the beautiful earth where we live.

God fills the earth

The earth was full of water, but God made land in the water and filled the land with rocks and dirt, plants and trees, valleys and mountains, rivers and fields. The earth was very beautiful.

God makes stars and planets

God filled the sky with stars and planets. He made the moon and the sun to give us light and warmth. Everything was in perfect balance.

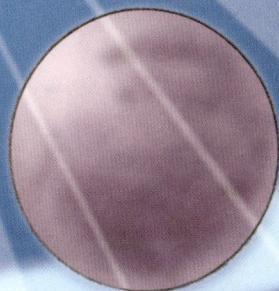

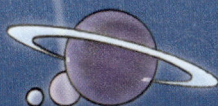

God makes animals

Now God wanted to make animals - animals that swim, animals that run and jump. God even made animals that climb trees, and animals that fly high in the air! They all loved the earth, and God loved the animals He had made.

God makes people

Then God wanted to make friends. He created a man and a woman that looked like Himself. The man He called Adam, and the woman He called Eve. God enjoyed his friends very much.

The garden of Eden

God made a special garden for Adam and
Eve. He called the garden Eden. In Eden,
no one was upset, and no one was fearful.
Eden was a friendly place, and God was
very, very happy with what He had made.

Creation in the Bible

Then God said, „Let us make man in our image, in our likeness, and let them rule over the fish of the sea and the birds of the air, over the livestock, over all the earth, and over all the creatures that move along the ground."

So God created man in his own image, in the image of God he created him; male and female he created them.

God blessed them and said to them, „Be fruitful and increase in number; fill the earth and subdue it. Rule over the fish of the sea and the birds of the air and over every living creature that moves on the ground."

Then God said, „I give you every seed-bearing plant on the face of the whole earth and every tree that has fruit with seed in it. They will be yours for food. And to all the beasts of the earth and all the birds of the air and all the creatures that move on the ground—everything that has the breath of life in it—I give every green plant for food." And it was so.

Genesis 1:26-30

NOAH'S ARK

Genesis 5:1 – 9:29

By faith Noah, when warned about things not yet seen, in holy fear built an ark to save his family. By his faith he condemned the world and became heir of the righteousness that comes by faith.

Hebrews 11:7

Evil people

God looked at the earth and saw how evil people had become. He felt sad because He wanted people to be happy and loving towards each other. So God decided to start all over again— with a man called Noah.

God tells Noah to build a boat

Noah was a good man. He loved God and wanted to do what God told him. Now God told him to build a boat.

"But there's no water around!" said Noah.

"You wait and see," said God. "I have decided to destroy the earth in a heavy rainstorm. You will soon need a boat."

God also told Noah to bring animals into the boat.

"You and your family and all the animals will be safe in the boat," God promised.

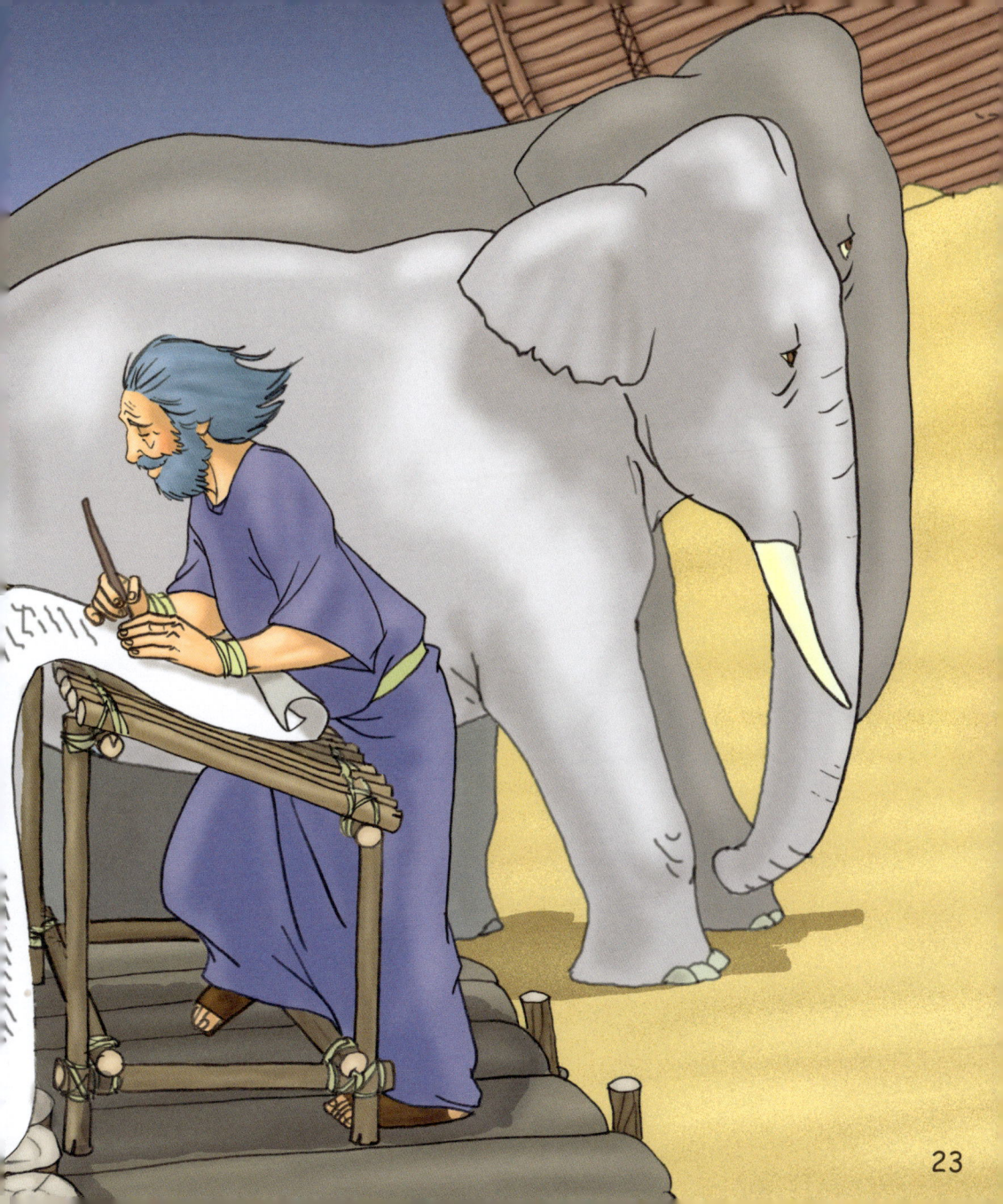

The rainstorm

Then it started to rain. Soon the water covered all the houses and high places where people were trying to escape the flood. Only Noah's boat was left.

The rain went on and on until the whole earth was covered with water. But Noah and his family and the animals were safe in the boat.

Inside the boat

It rained for forty days. In the meantime, Noah and his family were busy taking care of the animals.

Then the rain stopped. But Noah stayed on the boat for a long time until he thought the water had finally disappeared.

Noah sends out a dove

Before Noah let out the animals he wanted to be sure it was safe to get off the boat. So he sent out a dove. The dove came back with a green leaf. Now Noah knew there was dry land. It was safe for the animals to get off the boat.

God's rainbow

The animals spread out on the face of the earth, and Noah became the father of many people. God was happy and promised Noah never to destroy the earth again. As a sign of His promise He put a beautiful rainbow in the sky for everyone to see.

The rainbow reminds us that God loves us very much.

Noah's Ark in the Bible

The LORD then said to Noah, "Go into the ark, you and your whole family, because I have found you righteous in this generation. Take with you seven of every kind of clean animal, a male and its mate, and two of every kind of unclean animal, a male and its mate, and also seven of every kind of bird, male and female, to keep their various kinds alive throughout the earth. Seven days from now I will send rain on the earth for forty days and forty nights, and I will wipe from the face of the earth every living creature I have made."

And Noah did all that the LORD commanded him.
Noah was six hundred years old when the floodwaters came on the earth. And Noah and his sons and his wife and his sons' wives entered the ark to escape the waters of the flood. Pairs of clean and unclean animals, of birds and of all creatures that move along the ground, male and female, came to Noah and entered the ark, as God had commanded Noah. And after the seven days the floodwaters came on the earth.

Genesis 7:1-10

CHRISTMAS

Luke 2:1—21

34

For to us a child is born, to us a son is given, and the government will be on his shoulders. And he will be called Wonderful Counselor, Mighty God, Everlasting Father, Prince of Peace.

Isaiah 9:6

A special baby

One day an angel came to Mary and told her she was going to have a baby. "This is a very special baby," the angel said. "His name shall be Jesus and he will be the Son of God!"

As soon as the angel had left, Mary ran home to Joseph, her husband-to-be, and told him what the angel had said.

No room at the inn

Mary and Joseph were on their way to Bethlehem, a city far away. Mary was pregnant and was soon to have her baby. But when they finally came to Bethlehem, there was no room for them at the inn.

Born in a barn

The inn keeper told Mary and Joseph they could stay in the barn for the night.

This very night Jesus was born. God's own Son was born among cows and sheep in a barn in Bethlehem!

Shepherds in the field

In a field nearby, some shepherds were taking care of their sheep. Suddenly they heard singing, and as they looked up, the sky was filled with angels! The angels told the shepherds the good news that the Son of God had been born in Bethlehem.

43

Three wise men

Far away in the East, some wise men heard of Jesus' birth. They thought that Jesus must be a king and set out to see him. They followed the bright star all the way to Bethlehem until they came to the house where Jesus was.

Gifts to Baby Jesus

The shepherds and the wise men were very happy.
They knew this baby was the Son of God.
The wise men brought gifts to Jesus to show how
grateful they were to God.

The first Christmas in the Bible

In those days Caesar Augustus issued a decree that a census should be taken of the entire Roman world. (This was the first census that took place while Quirinius was governor of Syria.) And everyone went to his own town to register.

So Joseph also went up from the town of Nazareth in Galilee to Judea, to Bethlehem the town of David, because he belonged to the house and line of David. He went there to register with Mary, who was pledged to be married to him and was expecting a child. While they were there, the time came for the baby to be born, and she gave birth to her firstborn, a son. She wrapped him in cloths and placed him in a manger, because there was no room for them in the inn.

Luke 2:1-7

48

EASTER

John 20:1—31

Christ has indeed been raised from the dead, the firstfruits of those who have fallen asleep. For since death came through a man, the resurrection of the dead comes also through a man. For as in Adam all die, so in Christ all will be made alive.

1 Corinthians 15:20-22

Jesus and his friends

Jesus was a good man who helped many people. He had many friends, and his closest friends believed he was God's own Son. But there were others who didn't like Jesus. They talked behind his back of how they could get rid of him.

Jesus is arrested

Jesus' enemies wanted to have Jesus arrested and put to death. So they decided to catch him at night while he was alone with his closest friends. The soldiers brought him to a judge and demanded he be crucified on a cross. Most of Jesus' friends were afraid and ran away.

Jesus on the cross

Only a few of Jesus' friends were with him when he was nailed to the cross. They were very sad because they had hoped he would live forever. But Jesus died on Good Friday and they buried him in a grave outside the city of Jerusalem.

Jesus' enemies were happy. They thought they had finally gotten rid of him. To make sure he wouldn't come back they placed a huge rock in front of the doorway.

The angel and the soldiers

Outside the grave sat two guards. Suddenly
on Easter morning they heard a rumble and
saw an angel roll the stone away from the
grave. They had never seen an angel before, so
they got very frightened and ran off.

The empty grave

Later that morning, Jesus' friends came out to the grave to mourn his death. But what had happened? The grave was open and there was no Jesus in the grave! Where could Jesus be?

Jesus' friends were scared. They didn't know who had taken Jesus' body away.

Jesus is alive

As they turned to go home, they suddenly saw Jesus standing right in front of them! Now they understood that no one had taken Jesus' body away. Jesus had simply risen from the dead! Jesus was alive!

Jesus' friends were very, very happy. They hurried back to the others to tell them that Jesus was alive.